Other 'crazy' gigglebooks by Bill Stott
Sex – it drives us crazy!
Football – it drives us crazy!
Rugby – it drives us crazy!
Cats – they drive us crazy!

Published simultaneously in 2004 by Helen Exley Giftbooks in Great Britain, and Helen Exley Giftbooks LLC in the USA

12 11 10 9 8 7 6 5

Selection and arrangement copyright © 2004 Helen Exley
Cartoons copyright © 2004 Bill Stott
Design by 451° <studio@451.uk.com>

ISBN 978-1-86187-753-6

Printed in China

Helen Exley Giftbooks, 16 Chalk Hill, Watford, Herts, WD19 4BG, UK
www.helenexleygiftbooks.com

A HELEN EXLEY GIGGLEBOOK

Marriage

IT DRIVES US CRAZY!

CARTOONS BY BILL STOTT

"Done? I haven't done anything!"

"You don't understand...
I think Kylie's fantastic,
ultimately sexy, amazing – a goddess
– but I married you!"

"He thinks I love him for his come-to-bed eyes. **Actually** I'm crazy about the way he can't put shelves up."

"Well, if you haven't seen this show before, how come you rustle your paper in all the good bits?"

"Well, let's see – it's Tuesday... couple of months it'll be Christmas... it's not my birthday... Nope, I give up. What is it?"

"Ha! Playing hard to get, eh?"

"At half the price, it
would have looked
fantastic."

"Last week he promised to pay me a fine each time he forgot to put something away. By now, I could afford a new DVD!"

"Okay, there's something wrong
isn't there? I know the signs..."

"Casserole? Again?"

"So this big mean-looking kid walks up and says 'Gimme the bag'. And Gerry says 'Okay, punk, beat it', didn't you, Gerry?"

"And when he does come
to the supermarket, he's no help."

"George! Stop telling my joke!"

"Sorry about that, Darling,
 I didn't want to miss the goal.
 You were saying something about
 having an affair...?"

"There must be some mistake. We're in credit!

"Love might make the world go round but it doesn't make it any tidier!"

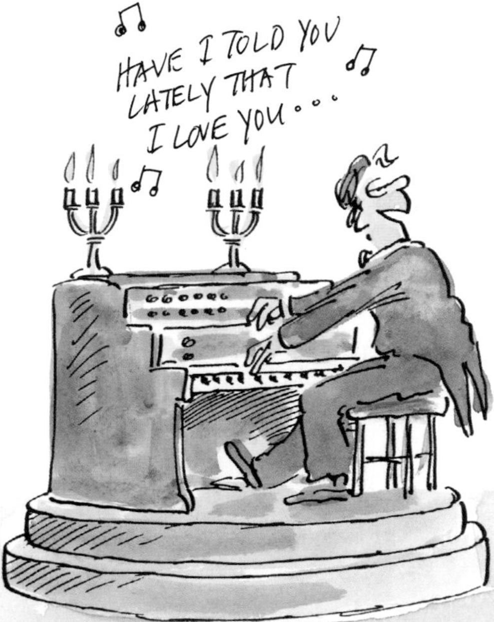
HAVE I TOLD YOU
LATELY THAT
I LOVE YOU...

"You might think it's full of olde worlde charm, but I'll tell you – after an hour every night for the last twenty-three years, maybe you'd find it a little tedious."

I LOVE YOU
MAVIS FENSTOOTH

LOVE YOU MAVIS FENSTOOTH!

YOU MAVIS FENSTOOTH!

MAVIS FENSTOOTH

About Bill Stott

Bill Stott is a freelance cartoonist whose work never fails to pinpoint the absurd and simply daft moments in our daily lives. Originally Head of Arts faculty at a city high school, Bill launched himself as a freelance cartoonist in 1976. With sales of 2.8 million books with Helen Exley Giftbooks, Bill has an impressive portfolio of 26 published titles, including his very successful *Spread of Over 40's Jokes* and *Triumph of Over 50's Jokes*.

Bill's work appears in many publications and magazines, ranging from the *The Times Educational Supplement* to *Practical Poultry*. An acclaimed after-dinner speaker, Bill subjects his audience to a generous helping of his wit and wisdom, illustrated with cartoons drawn deftly on the spot!

What is a Helen Exley giftbook?

We hope you enjoy *Marriage – it drives us crazy!*. It's just one of many hilarious cartoon books available from Helen Exley Giftbooks, all of which make special gifts. We try our best to bring you the funniest jokes because we want every book we publish to be great to give, great to receive.

HELEN EXLEY GIFTBOOKS creates gifts for all special occasions – not just birthdays, anniversaries, weddings and Christmas, but for those times when you just want to say 'thanks' or 'I love you'. Why not visit our website, www. helenexleygiftbooks.com, and browse through all our present ideas?

ALSO BY BILL STOTT
Cats – they drive us crazy!
Football – it drives us crazy!
Rugby – it drives us crazy!
Sex – it drives us crazy!

Information on all our titles is also available from
Helen Exley Giftbooks, 16 Chalk Hill, Watford WD19 4BG, UK. Tel 01923 250505